THE GRAND

POETRY COLLECTION

CREATED BY

CALEB JEFFREY GOREY

WITHOUT VALUE

WE RESORT TO FINDING GARDENS IN THE WILDERNESS

FUELED BY THE MOST NATURAL DESIRE

BUT STILL

WE GET LOST AGAIN AND AGAIN

TABLE OF CONTENTS

PART I

VENTURES FROM WITHIN

A DIARY FOUND DOWN

BY THE BEACH

APOSTLE

I

Here lie,

Personal thoughts grounded by internal gravity.

And here, through:

My being and composition of spirit and value.

To the celebration of something secretive and cold,

Something metallic in the leaves or-

Something draped in gold.

A party for something inhumane,

Is a party where the noon is cold,

Is a party without a name and no one has names,

Is a party for all of the gold.

A party during an evening,

I went there needing something only I wasn't feeling nothing-

At the door when I arrived.

I should have been leaving.

Temptation to feel and to crave an affair,

Made lights blaring piercing darkening-scenes-become darkening snares,

Where a girl met me finally,

Not while I sleep,

There was an incredible vibrancy.

And I gave up my need.

In reverse,

She moved as she repeated a verse.

All is so increasingly beautiful!

Hellish feels nothing of a curse,

The feeling was worse at five in the morning,

When I enthroned a new dream,

To imagine a better time,

Without jealous loanings.

A shimmering prime,

With big eyes,

And pastel flourishings.

Because Joseph craved for a reality that he could bend,

And Mary was too wild for this contingency to end.

And a devil planned to send an unaccepted hope,

That was to forget time and wasting it,

To support the mind and savor it.

Mary was like an apostle,

The devil dressed in gold to withhold-

Her responsibilities, and I met and I blessed them.

And her intentions were real,

I had no choice so I left them (goods).

I let them-

Believe fictional good,

Mary was like an apostle and she understood.

Mary was what I hold.

Breathing-

Releasing-

What God holds.

THE WINDY ISLAND

The day was colder than the week before. The wind and how there was no talking made it almost a bad thing.

We were standing all together in the morning when the stone mosaic beneath us and the rest of the world were all darkened at the edges and cursed at the shadows but enlightened in our gathering.

The absent of light was draining the blue,

Seeping opalescent baby blue just above the trees,

Across the lake.

But I was happy with it.

I was happy by the sky-saturation.

Even while I was freezing,

And alone holding my knees to my chest on the rocks,

And letting my mind fill with the evenings.

Unfortunately there was rage within the spectrum of my mind,

And the colors I saw heat and cool before me—

They leave my lungs and stomach empty,

I give up mine.

A spectrum we could feel ,

And the feeling was numb.

Red rainbows reign across the sky,

And across our arms,

Scare me into clearing my throat,

Laying in white sheets,

Forgetting gravity of us,

And we remain afloat on personal tendencies.

Flushed skin brushes,

Against thorns and branches that rushed sins

Erupted in the woods.

This hue was for her,

A new shade of sun.

An unseen but felt color.

I've written countless times-

Of her.

And countless I do breathe.

I've written of space,

And the gardens of death.

This is the dream I've been developing,

This is the truth:

Heat

A black hole that is enveloping.

It is the wandering and never mentioned girl,

Who understands the dream,

Who understands the world.

She understands the surge in my head,

The product of truth,

Not imagination.

Comprised within these winsome lines

Lies revoluting lines

About flaws in every composition,

Though, I know of and write of the truth,

I am a God

Left for me to behold

CEREMIC ARCHES

As I let the fires by night serve-

As a system of influence,

They die,

And so must I?

Absolutely against it,

For, I know in the morning I will be at that modern palace,

In which I find my way,

With my map—

An atlas.

High ceilings of earth tones,

smell of damp cement,

Taste of cold I meant to come a different day when the air was not so humid.

With no demand of the architecture,

The architect is still unable to represent himself.

As he is not used to any demand,

And his demand-

Was then theirs.

I arrive there by morning.

With no doors or windows or rooms.

The grey of morning and condensation freely accumulates around the palace,

And I have abandoned my atlas.

If this palace is the creation by purity without demand,

No properties exaggerated and excessive the-

Architect is fatted and he leaves his work-

In the middle of the field,

Under heavy grey fog.

The grey walls are abstract without all their smog,

But I am there and I let the monument consume I—

Believe this place is directed by the elite person's mind.

If no demand and no barrier of currency and no excessiveness and nothing of the world is put-

Into the palace,

Then this palace creates us.

And alone I abandon my facade.

And I feel the cement walls,

And as I let emotion become imbued with extravagant spirit,

My hands become pale and my mind becomes God.

THE VANILLA SANCTUARY

It is ultimately inadequate to assume gentle storms,

Of which dissolve into our normal bipolar mental forms.

To have surged within the depths of all that is gold,

There is a cold truth that exists beyond comprehension,

For it has been uncovered from it's early slumber-

Under a mess of what we have made.

I ventured to the beautiful vanilla sanctuary alone,

To find the flowers they said were from the heavens.

Aggravated mind-minds to the night and lets me be during the day.

The most vivid point of the day goes and I cannot find any flowers.

The clouds continue to move away from the sun,

And the moon is to come in thirteen hours.

Persuaded by honor,

I've been away from home for some time now.

Time is used experiencing the lusts time gives.

My eyes begin to hurt as I sleep to bring her back,

There is no traffic to disrupt my thoughts.

I began to slowly develop the truth that worrying is waste.

In this place we knew not each other,

To this haven I brought another-

Perspective of life that was to be uncovering this monument:

A mighty epiphany,

In the day where the sky kept to itself,

My heart resonated with the sound of the vanilla sanctuary.

I swear soon,

In this place it feels like we are treated like how kids treat the moon.

It is quiet within the fields,

By the lake there is no fake expression.

I wrote there about the assumed fate of the world.

Even during the day the architecture of this nature was increasingly smooth.

I had laid myself down near the dock where there was a garden,

The resemblance between this place and the grand sanctuary,

The difference between this waste and the honest death of me,

Is that there, there is beauty in happiness.

Beauty in evil-

Beauty in air-

Beauty in people.

It is the obvious composition of something that was never existing,

For which we wholly don't comprehend.

POWER LAKE

I

It was by the lake,

That morning in the north.

Early when the pines weren't awake,

Five hours after midnight,

The fourth.

Air condensed behind the fabric of her sweater,

Vanilla white,

Cobalt blue,

Grey heather.

The air above was sharp and cold against her face and skin.

She would go to the forest in steam,

Looking beyond that rosy place,

Feeling the sand and the sin scraped-

Burning in the same place.

The sun and the wind rushed through the tall trees,

The beach that cradles the metal lake.

She was down in the sand,

Crying into the lake,

On her knees.

SUMMER CAMP

Look up to-

Vivid mountains and rocky cathedrals,

Concurring forests and their primeval.

Sweet in smell,

A land where the fields all float.

Near the fire by night she gave me a note,

Quiet embers burning beneath the strings,

Bodies dissipate-

As one of us sings:

Oh, they're beams of light

Silent was the war in the night

Feelings that could be the fire

Embers surging so higher

Feeling the revealing of love brought with each strum.

We reach for another that writes under the same sun.

Fireside, we hold each other

Burning were the trees above when they caught on fire,

And so did I when I found out that you lied.

Because becoming the best for you was all that I've-

Spent my time trying to do.

I've dedicated my mind,

I've gotten rid of them,

Oh, I've gotten rid of my mind.

Never sleeping in your bed,

I wake up at three,

Only to fall asleep with my mind awake.

A castle of blankets around us,

On top of the rock,

With a bloody knee,

With our feet in the lake.

Their roaring lungs,

Sore to indulge,

To be was my heart that she allowed for.

To need liquor,

She knows me-

For,

Believing this drowned thought was the key.

Sober clouds were haunting me,

But I let my self be chained down,

It's some sort of free anyways.

The grass is too long,

I cannot feel you,

Nor,

Can I see.

I dreamt of more.

Below me was the Manitoba Diamond Lake's shore,

Confined by the wild rain.

Waking up with lesser pain and seeing her,

Walking to where the sun came through.

The proof of time I completely forgot,

Quietly mindless, walking where the dark grass was still damp.

We breathed this untouched air,

And found ourselves at summer camp.

NOT NEARLY DARK

5:24 AM

The sky this morning was increasingly smeared and numb to the colors: pink, red, and steel blue. I studied it carefully, as to wonder about the blue and where it changed. This nature was so compelling to me; shadows casted from the dense canopies above and behind me had been untouched by daytime and were still very cold. Only the shaking spots of golden light that appeared on the ground from between the leaves above allowed for warmth. And so I saw this real beauty of raw nature as it was all still asleep and unseen by anyone else, yet. Seeing and smelling paired well together on this walk. The experience was comforting; autumn is her favorite of the seasons.

Only it wasn't *her.* No, my Love wasn't with me, but this frontier of beauty I walked through reminded me of another. Being confronted by the end of the trail and an opening of land so glorious punctured some extremity and nervousness into my chest; yes, the ultimate feeing? I felt the depth of my lungs, as if I was scared of heights and myself being above. But the feeling was much too similar to how I felt when I first met her. How is it the tightness of my skin and the cold air augments these heavy feelings? Oh, how the ghosts were us and we knew not each other but the clothes we wore around our arms, necks, and chests. No, she roamed not with us, and god knows what she was doing at home. No. I went with three others that were draped in thick sweaters and scarves and knew to devour the morning in silence. And everyone knows that this was the only way to devour the morning.

The trail was a steady incline through the Northern Ontario wilderness, where the leaves upon the ground were icy and the air could not be healthier. The hollow trail shot through the woods and climbed until it ended and the trees faded away.

I was second to stray away from the forest and see the natural plateau of land at the head of the hill.

Together we stood in the middle of flat land, only it wasn't just a clearing. The place behind us contributed to the beauty, somehow. Behind us was the magnificent face of a mountain that began down behind at a valley hidden by thick woods. The trail may have branched off and visited that valley.

Before us was this complete view of the worlds' apex perfection. We were quite high up, there on that plateau, and we had no idea.

Or maybe we did, for my routined breathing felt dangerous, scratching up and down my lungs, as winter could provide that same brutality. And I second-noticed that. I subconsciously attempted to dismiss the feeling of the air, but could not. I believe it was the natural limitation of my mind—I could not suppress.

There were no thoughts on where the sun could be then, though it was bright, it did not matter where it was. Too far behind the mountain, maybe. The day only matured the longer we stood, so we went on back through the woods that were shadowed dim, but not for long, and not nearly dark yet.

VOLLEY

40°

Kentucky

I had begun settling for the heat of the place, and thought less of it throughout my stay. It was as dreadful as it was consistent. In real life, the thickness of the air maintained it's promise to keep us seemingly miserable. Eventually we adapted and all was fine, but not immediately so.

To stimulate the parts of our minds that desired relief, it was provided by nature in a metaphorically medicinal way; we waited. And for: The time between the dark of night and the dyings of day. Personally, I thought nothing more of the light than for it to be equal with whatever can be dark. Given the dimming of the place in the afternoon made certain others feel much more comfortable with themselves and their display. Then, days were nothing more of time and life was just how we wasted it.

I hadn't anything to do this one evening, and I never spent a lot of time by the lake we neighbored. The sky behind me could not settle its excited metallic gold color and seemed to melt towards the tree line before me. The sun sat behind streaks of pink crested altocumulus clouds that seemed so thin and whimsical.

I was immensely satisfied by the beach itself. I've never seen the water so calm, rid of those mad kids.

The beach was separated from the rest of the camp by tall trees with full and low branches. Kids began walking from the beach back to camp because of the time. It was becoming late, and they needed to sleep. I wasn't mindfully ready with leaving yet. So I stayed by a dead and a dry tree near the water, and no one ever saw me. I wanted to see the sun set one final time before my departure in the morning.

As the day fell this evening in Kentucky, I sat with one other wild animal as to admire the lake; she accompanied me. We sat together on the tree-corpse next to the dry one still standing that I had hid behind earlier. Across the cooled sand on the beach the light from some faraway fire glowed through the netting of a volleyball net.

(Interlude)

A young life, which in this case is my own, dismounts its theories that can *not* be solved.
By her, not a god, more-so death or the devil than a god, I was able to turn my perspectives and influenced (by her) ideologies into something-malleable.
For if it is malleable, it can be bent to reason and melted to a solution. Then, it is a theory,
and it can stay because it is true, and a reality at that.
The new coming of mind turned some vile and corrupt idea that everything is increasingly doomed, into something, beautifully, enabling advantages to myself.
I was convinced this was okay.
Of course, everything that ever was had to happen, and right after the pain or laughing,

It was okay.

Some could say it was baneful and wrong,

And troubled and conflicting,

Or depressing and hurting.

But it was truly the realer mindset, and by being so honest with the structures of spiritual

practices, societal tendencies, and everything else between literature and small, pointless science.

Well I could just take advantage of this knowledge which is—

This awareness.

I associated myself with her, whose intentions mirrored that of a goddess and whose appearance

contributed to mood and then, allure.

Oh, how isolation rid me of desire for young allure, and gifted me with this fascination with

philosophical allure.

And the setting, everything in a place, meant absolutely *everything* to *my* life.

So within a room:

Although the aura within the room and around our heads seemed appreciative of Chiaroscuro,

She was only trouble near the end. I mistook happiness with the happiness of others.

I forced myself to please others. Not this one, like this new girl.

She was the weapon I needed to rebel with this new realization and further establishing it. I knew

I wasn't wrong. But if I stated such, then I would be *obviously* wrong to them.

She was to revive my lost life no matter the cost and no matter the complications. What did she

say?

What did this girl who thought like a god, knew of everything, and appreciated beauty within

Infinitely small dimensions bring for me?

Then, she told me stories and what calms her mind and keeps her on this planet-

That she claims is how everyone should feel, right from the beginning of time.

That's how we began.

We kissed in the garden,

Listening to the rush of all the blood in our heads in the cold.

I told you I'd rather not feel pain anymore,

"You won't feel anything in all this cold"

Colors pour into and but don't mix with the red.

The sound of nothing feels humid,

In humane,

Arms and their chains shift through the bed.

We kissed in the garden.

I told her I craved some new beginnings,

Braving raved winnings.

An empty night lined with neon lights,

Surely all that is beautiful is capable of sinning?

And so, why do it in the first place?

DINING IN A HEAVENLY LIT ROOM

DREAM I

Mary, now couldn't we breathe in that smooth air for a while?

Take back these seven layers,

I don't care much for these monsters who cry but attempt to still smile.

The world is burning but it isn't here. Beyond the crest of our clothes we fear-

Nearing the end of our story.

I wrote this for you,

I wrote of the blue.

Your body just lies-

About the future and hope.

Her body just lies-

About the future and hope.

We had made some new plans to see each other. This was, I believe, a couple months into the year and it was actually spring. But it was still fairly cold outside and the streets were clean and there wasn't any snow or mud. She came to my house and from there I drove, but we may have walked, to some restaurant that doesn't exist but I swear I've seen the architecture before. The entrance was a windowless wooden door about ten feet high. Inside it smelt like an empty house that was just painted, and there was a draft. The walls were a whitish color but had very light baby blue paisley decor all along the walls which ran all the way up to a glossy wooden ceiling that was ridiculous in itself. There were even marble pillars in between circle tables. The tables were all white with flawless wine glasses along with all white tables and silverware. It was all untouched and there were multiple tables occupied by older people. We felt special there, you were in a black dress I was in a typical suit with a pearly tie. The waiter was kind and we ate some food that I don't remember. The building was crammed, it was skinny and bright from natural light that came through windows that never were.

DAY ONE:

BY THE LAKE AND NOT THE BONFIRE

11:47 tonight,

She is no hell,

She is my heaven in spite—

Of my feeling of lonesomeness sometimes.

Feel my index finger and thumb under your chin.

A sun will never set-

With a lover's hands,

Every night the stars melt unto her rib cage skin.

Illuminated neon rings around eyes look away-

To a blue distant ocean wave under day.

Are you with me?

Beyond the dark of the universe,

How it peaked over a horizon's infinity vibrance.

I held her until after midnight,

She asked-

All shivered.

Held me,

We'll bathe in the moonlight.

I called her responsible for my Destiny,

Like the nature of state, her mind was extra heavy.

Traced on my skin, my ached veins,

Without a pen but tracings from a skinny finger and the nail of it-

Spelled her own name.

The same finger traced the sun,

Like art within a frame.

I would never let her go,

We never continued our orbit.

Bronze eyes dripped with insanity,

And the wind of the fall night hums.

Unalterable tongues bound together by audible weight-

tangle themselves about,

when she comes.

APOSTLE

II

In that bed I felt like Neptune,

Slivers as lines that're blue along my chest.

I let the natural days' light in so you can see the beauty as I do.

And when we can see the same beauty exist in the natural light,

And in the darkened mornings and cool nights,

We have feelings closing to collide in between light and dimness.

And eventually I may tell you I died a long time ago.

Only so I could find the entire hell,

But still,

An entire truth,

And expel myself from this suffering—

Someone great told me about—

The idea of you caused this,

But left my mind coloring.

It is,

Astronomical bliss is the idea that-

Comets never miss—they eventually hit something.

And in the horizon I saw Death's kiss,

I saw a girl stop my days.

But the whatever good drains so quickly when Death comes back,

Fraying sleeves of mine,

Death lives,

And the trusted pain I did would never leave.

That night,

I dreamt of hills

I swallowed the pills with pale skin when I woke.

Lamp lights beamed along my wrists,

As I inhaled that unholy smoke.

Broken was this bond between the apostle and Death,

The end of all by the burning of her seductive breath.

Stretching sunsets—her scanning hands did me in,

As the sun sets in my head, and it's increasingly dim.

When I look at you the feeling is inevitably unfathomable

Skin felt by skin surely is the purest,

When the ocean would begin at the sand and blue,

A lover named Death,

Of which I told her:

It's you.

Ultimately full stars,

And the nature beneath presented by her

Far away she saw gold blood flood into veins

As the seductive Death prevails to numb any pain,

He carries on with better pain.

MARY

Mentioned to me,

Beautiful futures,

But current atrophy.

In royal graves: her thoughts remained.

In the nights of it I quickly subside myself,

And ignore her heating cries:

Comfort but surreptitiously showing her oppression-

As soon as I see her eyes.

Someone who loves tries methodological passages from her past experiences.

Mary,

An apostle,

Hopelessness resorts to metaphorical flashes and masses,

So to make me forget about my own past,

She saddens me alas-

At her heavy and great gate,

Where reality and fiction crash.

SNEAKING TO THE OBSERVATORY ON THE HILL

Discovering what drives her

Into insanity

A beautiful theory you wish could be

Proven in sanity.

Her eyes are described to have a common constellation

Too beautiful and far

But connected at intentions in the sky and then down to our wrists.

A tale told by astronomers with great minds

Who lay and watch the sky for speeding stars

As quiet recidivists.

She falls beneath blues

Into a limbo so bleak

But grand at the same time

Into an ocean of her own tears

Her theory stated she was fine and woven into fairytale tongue-ties

Stories about drowning into an abyss

That subside at the bottom of this:

We develop ideas and theories by the pond on the hill only in matured day

And we leave when the blue lowers to black and for an hour we'd have nothing to say.

A mind begins to leave.

It's on the outside-beside me.

Her ways of old folk tales

Made some eyes wide

She was so sad once

So much that her feet left the ground

Drifting away from her place

The opposite of Hell bound.

Until some day

We'd all believe she'd fallen from the clouds.

Her smile left no crescent in the sky

There was no more rain that showered

Everything

And darkened

She'd return to her bed.

No sun

Dried.

He took her home to his house

She fell asleep on his chest.

He knew he'd never want to part

The constellations

Of which he might have designed-

and wrote the rest.

INTERLUDE

I

Breath is fogging up the glass

I'll take you out of here tonight

Until there's fire by day

The hymn was your moan at night

We rely on the woods

The howling fever was known too well

I'll take care of you

When the bags under your eyes begin to swell

The sun is there but we can't see it

Fingertips like silver linings

Peeking over the sky's edge

The black was malleable

And I could feel it

Fire of;

There's an endless oblivion

The constellations fall limp to the floor

 Of which mirrored life as-

We don't dream anymore

FINALE, THE BEAR

I never heard her calling,

Sounds nothing more of the Sirens.

She was all cobalt,

Under rain shimmering.

By our hearts go-

Powered with vigor,

A week spent,

Waking up to nothing warm.

Yet,

So was such deprived love anyway,

In which we crave colors like gold,

Or the tone of any day.

One craved time,

I thought she was that,

Few traced bold lines

Cold times upon my skin and that-

She nearly begins:

Four more days.

By the fire:

What ignites yours?

But I didn't say her,

And she didn't speak.

I said to them that mine was nature,

S'il vous plaît laissez,

For another week.

Through the woods getting blisters,

From climbing that mountain with Her.

The air was cooler-

Up there,

But our chests and hands are hot because we're called-

Sinners.

No, there was the least desire to win her that night,

The wind was too much,

Obligated to hold her tight.

I told my love,

I missed her.

Under the stars I kissed her

But they moved fast

That won't heal

They all asked

But we're okay.

She breathed fire

In the long grass—we had a field day

Wind threw our clothes—over

Her hair flew

Ten days over.

You couldn't get mad

This was all you

Perfection battles hell

In noise

This was your choice.

I told my love,

I missed her inside the tent

I kissed her

Above the ground

Some grandeur

Like our weakest knees

Wilder thrilling her.

I told my love,

I missed her.

Down by the creek

Cannot breathe

Blood sped down over our freezing,

Uncharted and lesser composed

The windy island reimposed

She said some words

But the rain was too loud

She knows the dreams

Fade on the beach,

Cream beams stream along her cheeks,

Coat the eyes

Promising their weather is clearer

Though the clouds are thick.

They had no idea,

We were both drained in mind on the cliff.

I think it might be over soon

Her eyes were obsidian marbles

And her mind was like the moon.

I read to her the song of wolves and home

She whispered to make room

She didn't understand why the wolves,

They lay in their monochrome.

Her knuckles were pale and her nails were silver

I held them when the stars went.

She sleeps as-

She knew the bear could kill her.

I read to her about something I made-up.

How these wolves cannot not deprive us

If we're divided for long enough by bears who care hard enough.

You mustn't fall asleep to them

I told her

We cannot fall lifeless again by ourselves

Or together.

Behind the masses we could

But the fires were out

We leave the wilder,

Falling down the hillside,

Deprived, but she cannot fair-

As I write the finale,

About a bear.

INSIDE A VICTORIAN HOUSE

The floors creek once again,

Shadows blare behind me like curtains,

They dance because the wind is loud.

It's so freezing inside the victorian house.

Fallen upwards to the attic,

That's where the ever so vivid happened.

Every movement would make the floors under us creek,

But I was focused on the poisonous kiss making the vigorous weak.

Years there,

Stack upon my years.

I sit surrounded by purple dust,

With a window across showing me the lake,

The course floorboards under me-

Begin to ache.

The boy and the girl,

Who's hearts start to flood,

Shatter in attics,

Dripping in intoxicated blood.

Our drying and freezing-

Floorboards keep up their creaking,

The attic is bathed in something like blood,

And blanketed by snow.

Winter is upon the warmth,

When the sun will soon wake up-

And enlighten a fiery glow outlining the distant white tree-line.

The boy returns to the attic,

In desire to feel that cold again.

The light drips through a tiny crack,

Dropping his heart in metaphor,

That he could not mend again.

The boxes and their shadows in a bleak stance,

He slips through the floorboard,

Dust rains below,

Into the wind.

The lines and limbs; they dance like the curtains.

SOON IT WILL BE COLD ENOUGH

Soon it'll be cold enough,

For the storm in your heart to surge to another.

It'll be cold enough for the aching to stop,

My love,

I know it's been aching for a while.

Your hair will freeze when the sky becomes cobalt;

Brunette hair that becomes white when the snow falls.

Her lungs fill up and become in need of a smoke,

She slowly breathes "I love you " but she never spoke.

The sweater sleeves have become torn and stained with grape and cherry.

He loves her eyes but they're beginning to flood.

Soon it'll be cold enough,

For chapped lips to become warm again.

It'll be cold enough for the forests to comfort you,

My love,

I know you've felt stranded.

Her dimples will grin and her teeth will show,

The moccasins begin to disappear beneath the snow.

The branches reach out to grab your ankles,

Baby turn back,

This isn't new; we are in shambles as we are falling a part every time-

I begin the preamble, love!

It's too cold for us here, all I'm ever hearing is sadness that isn't thought-through!

She promised him she wouldn't go anywhere without you!

I'm becoming faster,

But the darkness had been upon her already.

At the abandoned house,

Hereafter.

Collapsing under her own two feet.

The ice—she couldn't see—had been kept to us-

Discreet.

Fallen into the ice below.

Her bloodied lip drips soaking into the snow.

She'd pull herself away from this rut,

She'd let him believe,

Unlikely she'd lie.

Like her skin was uncut?

She was only embarrassed.

Soon it'll be cold enough,

For the winter contingency to go into us.

It'll be cold enough for her hands to grow numb,

My love,

I know they've been burning.

THE CRASH

Astronomical feelings inside her mind,

An atmosphere kept her mind content.

Her hair flew to the buoyancy of gravity,

Saturn was thrown right at me,

And all of its consent.

She feels colder now,

She lowers her left brow,

To let me know how she meant.

A storm of controversy casted over me,

And she was questioning her state of mind.

A new scratch bound upon her left cheek,

The glass danced and was left behind,

As we create a new scene when she questions her state of mind.

Inside she's dying now,

Her lungs will soon collapse,

Within the atmosphere she has now created—

The years will then relapse.

Deep into the universe you can find her,

Behind the brightest sun,

Slowly lying and denying,

That she's the only one.

Her body rejoins the Earth,

And her atmosphere shatters into the dancing glass,

Blooded tears fill her eyes,

Water concusses the crash.

Now, the life escapes her eyes,

And she believes that she survived,

And that it was not that she cried, nor did she cry the ocean prior.

Swim to the top,

The instant stop,

Riveting grinding sounds underneath the surface,

And glares from the fire.

Sirens cry with her to compensate,

The fact that those astronomical feelings in her mind,

Are still there.

Not on the moon,

But in her lungs.

The water drowns her.

She's woken me up.

LAKES OF MAHOGANY

I can smell the tea from the kitchen,

Golden sunlight shows a beautiful ocean around the pupil of her eyes.

I can hear the leaves in the trees outside,

It was our alarm,

She left the bed.

Each step made the floor creek,

And the sound woke me up so I followed her.

I'd be led outside where she wasn't to be found,

The leaves were dancing unto the patio and off of it.

The leaves left and now I could see her,

Her beautiful shape facing the lake of mahogany.

Her hair was thrown in the wind.

I walked to her,

The leaves were spinning and scrapping,

She was gone.

My love inhales her fire by the fire,

The lowering of the night lays upon us;

The stars appear and melt into our mouths.

Skin illuminated,

Tight,

By fire and by the fire.

Silver embers searing the skin on my shins and sometimes my collarbone.

Diamonds speckled above her cheeks shiver and drip.

Some distance away from the fire-

The air felt like ice.

Opalescent glass eyes,

A sun died out at the time.

A second came lipped,

Overlaid by one castle-cloud.

Turning within us,

In motion.

Four lying,

Saying there was lust.

But the ocean falls from the sky,

As some sort of luck.

I left her holding,

And kept to myself in the thunder-shack.

Not feeling-

Any kind of luck as I still do not have her,

But if I never do have her,

That must be okay.

But I do only have the rest of the week.

Devouring the night,

As I revolt:

My love, who is still back home.

Insisting her stay in my mind,

A nightmare clawing my head:

A monster above the bed.

Waking up to a morning so dark,

And only the sun for time,

Maleficent lines of gold on her back-

—arches.

Everything is glowing,

Everything is cold-

Under the sheets.

Under the blue we're-

Secretly ultramarine

Whispers of thin clothes that-

—I cannot see.

Change by the tide,

She tells me she'll take in water-

By the sapphire sea.

Beyond the cerulean islands

Loving in a time where there were no stars

Salt abundant air

Salt abundant scars

When the day dissipated

It was the sky

Not me-she was gripping

Holding me

She was tripping turning

Tides within the bed

—were dripping

A pressure against my back

My head was a crane and I looked up

A view I seemed to lack my focus

I saw myself drip with steam

Gold in my eyes

Streams flowed down my face

Like blood when slaughterings are in play.

GOLD BILLION, AN ELITE PARTY

DREAM II

It was only Her though,

She asked if I was okay.

We began out of the amber-chrome room.

She was cloaked in a red velvet dress that hung around her arms,

Wrapped around her legs.

My hair matted like clay,

And her legs-

Around me soon,

When we'd dance.

It was if not for the wind that slid past my ears,

Nails laid around my waist.

Upon these vanilla clouds I would jump off the ledge of this tower near.

Devexity of glass on the side of this place,

He talked to me.

Nevertheless an actor.

I stared behind him at a gold sea,

And reconsidered my stay.

PART II

OF HEAT

AND OF GOLD

AS WE GO

FUJI

Silver of the clouds dripped into the river

Cold of the morning in the mountains

I told myself to not shiver

In the valley we slept through the exhaust of the day

Light traveled slowly in a seductive way

Under thick wool covers we lay pieced together

Until she picked me apart the next night and

Leaves die above in the blue sky—looking like feathers

Up and up the birds take flight

Smoke fills in a dimmed room lit with morning-saved light.

It was the intention of my first stare,

It was a beautiful expression.

I hold this lover with-

Metallic hands.

Light peels from the dimples on her back,

Pools of radiance overflow.

Golden lines low and appear slow-

Over her curves and bend she is-

Ever—glowing—radiance,

Troubled where the world ends for me.

NEARING THE END OF MACHAPUCHARE

It was last night she told me

A torch was leaving light along the garden path

Early morning and the end of the day

Lovers stand in our way

Bodies filled with holy wraith.

Vibrant was the one and the blossoms that sat in the water

Fields of color and all

Where the leaves began to fall

Spending all of these days asleep in unimaginable light.

The bloom of a nebula

Found deep in a hollow heart

Deep in character

Even in the picked-a-parts.

Is normality to be bitter and miserable

Or is reality miserably irrisistable?

Spending years alone

And content with indecision

The path to rid myself of suffering

Confined within the fundamentals of a garden's vision

A collision of kissings of each flower alone

Laying amongst the fuchsias where she picks me a part

PLUTO, THE FLOWER

I've lost who I am

In the stomach of mountains

All alone

As if her lips were so cold

And made of stone

She's all I ever needed

I wanted happiness that was consistently warm

But it comes to me still

In natural form

Time was melting away

In the morning we touched

Pain pouring with the ocean spray

The skin of Her arms were slightly flushed

Gifted with a shade brighter than any sun

Across mountains

Colors maintain their entirety and purity

As they are untouched by street lights

But a thousand suns could never compare to her eyes

Saturn rings along her thighs

As the sun peers through the blinds

With empty stomachs

We keep ourselves blind

In the middle of the night

Fingers stripped of their holy knowing

And taught by flaws

That're prior showings.

I saw her go

Last night—to

In the garden she sleeps

A flower

Pluto.

EVENINGS AT STEPPE FALLS

Close to closing my eyes now,

Out on the rocks.

Hand down to me,

Pisces,

The vernal equinox.

I used to know you,

Along the seaside at least.

Against the glass,

Half-done poems pouring from me;

Where the demons laugh and bad thoughts recede.

There is no place better to crave,

Than her arms.

in sane.

But the clouds collapse to snow just after the winter,

Slowly her curves move out of place.

I have welcomed her here.

It's the world I fear,

An epiphany I named,

She claimed:

A truth about happens and achieving it and pacifism.

And for her I crave.

Down to the falls,

Or to the beginning at the top,

We stopped and then walked on the side.

Exhausted

But we'll make it to the falls.

PARRY SOUND

We go to the harbor,

Just to leave the house,

And to see for-

Ourselves-

If the grey above and of the ocean,

Can strain our doubts.

Her name?

The birds sing it every morning,

In every story I read before bed,

In the psalms of the day.

So calming—

As I rest my head,

My jaw is numb.

How her lips were blue

And her eyes were red.

Unlaced ropes around shoulders of

Untied people that met and are barely friends

In the house she sang to him

This last night before he would go with her

As this is not the end

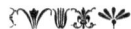

WILDER WRISTS I

And she goes through the Garden to find one to share her secret,

Fuchsias spread in the low season,

Under the violaceous skies she found her reason.

Drenched where the unhumanized air cleans,

Royalty perfected in the hands of this lover,

Sleeping in drifting currents of iridescence ,

il est mort dans ses rêves

Wilder Wrists

RICH EXHAUSTION

Laying lifeless over each-other,

Under plaid blankets we're covered.

Heat of palms.

Legs entangled and ashes smothered,

The ocean appeared like a sheet of diamonds,

Dark and unfathomably shuddered.

The air was cold and rushed in sound,

Quiet is my mind but in hers it was loud.

She had lightning hair that flourished under a silver sky,

Admiring the coming rapids,

Above the sapphire sea the birds fly and mess up the sky.

With her in my arms,

I think of another life.

Embracing the salty air;

Course as mine,

I fall wayward to blue eyes' stare.

The harbor was silent,

She was an angel that God sent.

Since her body was rich with allure,

The sun was gone and the moon was a crescent.

WILDER WRISTS II

Crimson fingernails wrote about the coast:

Poetry she adored the most.

Over the wind I heard her calling,

In your arms, I swear I'm in a garden!

And with our eyes closed we adore-

All that is made of gold.

And we hold,

Each-other when the hills become the floor.

Our lines intend to bend the fabric,

Of understanding relationships between sleeves and bends of rivers,

By them we become increasingly phatic:

I don't feel the ship sway as we go on anymore

The anchor, her body, and the sail have all gone,

May they wash up on shore?

Or sink to the bed,

In which I lay already?

I smell her breath,

With every morning we kiss.

Listening to the sound of the ocean,

Hold each other's shivering wilder wrists.

Writing about how one welcomes-

And another or both never repel.

She persuades me to love her,

Not somebody else.

Frayed in rain and we hoped for better weather,

Drifting into deep violaceous storms,

Hands intertwined in her sweater.

Assuming a flume of bedimmed forests that pour out to lakes,

Flowing to a hindrance.

She takes her shoes off once the condensation influences the not-so-black grass.

Eyes had fixated onto a violet and black setting,

Seeing a tempest crawl to the other side of the earth,

Feeling as if the storm was above us.

Relieving pressure within the air,

Paying others no mind,

So they incorporate their hellish snare.

Miserable under a night,

Gladly raining upward.

'Oh love'

'Give up'

Paying the Devils no mind.

DIVENIRE PLAYED AT THE YARD FOR THE PRINCESS

Mortality is in no courtyard,

Screaming inside-into another's arms,

Is wanting more important than need?

Death would never concede if-

She held onto me.

Needn't you lie to me but still-

She held onto lies before me.

Covered in black leaves,

Drenched in red sun,

Burning blues shine where my skin was pink.

Come down from the balcony my Love,

Oh please.

You've taught me:

Realism becomes romanticism,

As contemplated in isms.

I've called you,

A dichotomy of a soul,

Creation of stars,

That weren't new.

A fury of matter,

Falling from the skies.

And our fingertips don't get enough blood,

They feel like ice,

And my pupils widen,

When I stare into your eyes.

I was waking up and she's already here.

The air was cold,

Where the nape of her neck was bare.

Dressed in gold like a king,

Bronze was the metallic of her hair.

Her ghostly arms were burning between the sheets,

Written by eyes and what you told me two nights ago.

In the evening we comprise.

She despised lies,

So much she'd cry,

Over a truth when she found it,

So she pried-

Open a new ending.

Because the beginning was never-ending,

Written by eyes,

Dripping from her hands,

Sleeping,

God sighs,

Hell,

I get so lost in my head,

Every single time.

These damned feelings are embedded though,

I can't manifest them in my bed though.

Hungry for vigor—new holy throwings,

Kissing lips that never truly know of me.

Darling I'm going to let you go to,

Monsters Whose Eyes Subtly Glow.

You're behavior under these-

Florescent lights are low.

Creases begin to show underneath,

Dragged love until the sky is indigo,

She kept screaming my name,

Art

As if she thought she was kissing Van Gogh.

Love's getting in the greenhouse,

I grew hearts to convince my demons

She'd come in behind me and I had not known,

So I breathed in the humidity.

Destroyed 'till surface bound,

Together we'll write an ending to this,

Individually we crave some hellish and pretty sound.

MANITOBA

Condensation built up around her knees.

Day One allowed for time to think,

I no longer miss her,

And I have seven days to finally sleep,

I ask the French girl in the morning if-

I'm justified being happy alone.

A dragging other begins to leave my mind,

As I begin to good-dream-seamlessly of something dramatic-

And impossible.

Save me from the world you've shown me without-

Showing me.

My love, of course it's beautiful,

It's hurting now though,

Burning these gardens.

There's new pain in the passion that I convinced you to feel,

My love still brings me to her golden room to seduce.

This is all for you; to taste what is real,

It's like we're the only one,

I've been trying to tell you baby. This is it. Oh God it's wonderful. Come with me, you said you

wanted to be,

Holy.

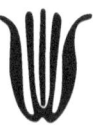

WATERFALLS OF CHISMS

It's forever we lie,

Extremes we cover that thrive by night.

We waste ourselves-

As we forget nature.

Extremity confides within a better place.

A place we shouldn't meet,

A place we shouldn't stay.

Dreams drip all over the bed,

Under the sheets.

Knowing you're out there;

A dream so concrete.

This ideology is comprised of a truth we both know,

To flow through gold skies,

`till rivers align,

To allow yourself to experience ultimate truth of mind,

Truth of life.

To dine with thoughts,

And produce shivers down the one's spine.

For, this truly is it,

And I am the end.

I've gained the most valuable materials,

By giving up all of my friends.

All so that I may understand the forgotten original purpose of life,

For, I've found that I,

Am alone to this campsite.

For, these increasingly useless friends have been.

And when I reach the end of the game of life,

Out by the waters,

I can look up to damp blue sky and then-

The smoke clouds above begin to bend.

POWER LAKE

II

Good Morning

July 10th 2015

Alone between stone cathedrals—

I heard the wind soaring.

The way I am loaning—

To a devil in my head that shares the same tongue.

I got out from the water,

And ignored the drenched clothes pressed against my back.

It had been raining for two days,

And we slept by the water under the canopies.

Lightning lighted a depressed and heavy sky,

The sound of pouring promised that we would never be dry.

I found her diary on the surreptitious island,

I tried to read her name but the ink bled through the backsides of the pages.

The day's epilogue was an abrupt and vicious end,

Much of it was lost in the storm.

Reading these wayward passages,

It never cleared but upon the cliff there was a consuming view.

There was this one night inside of our tent,

The sky was black but we could see the stars.

Most were asleep and we tried to wake them all,

And surge through the dark to the descent.

We came to the opening where the lake became space,

On the edge of that inevitable place.

Soft moonlight wrapped over chests,

You worried this moment would not be the best.

We fell into the water but to us it was glass,

A black mass,

But we had laughed anyways.

Until we reached the grass and got out,

Against the sky our eyes and the stars were an opalescent contrast,

Before the black mass.

In the morning the lake was still,

Smooth.

While we slept—

My heart had learned to kill three hours before.

It was cold this morning,

My eyes were heavy,

My happiness couldn't ever be fake.

Within the Manitoba wilderness,

We found Power Lake.

FLEUR PRÉFÉRÉE

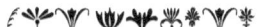

Explique

They wrote that she goes,

Where she goes—

Descends into rivers' flowing to us.

Slowing shivers come—

Early in the day,

No one knows—

I am out there,

That day.

Sweaters fraying,

Where the cuffs of her sleeves,

At their ends.

Elbows bend before,

And her hands,

They descend—

Over ice.

The heart-heat that melts us,

Generate the excited waves in our heads,

And under our lungs,

Annoyance to suffice.

Stir the river bed,

The black sand on the shore of paradise,

Subsiding at the floor of my mind.

Pastel days overthrew—

Faded haze.

In ablaze we lay in the bed,

In the blue,

It was only a phase,

It's always—

Making us feel lesser during the day.

And for our nights,

However,

We feel the most at the nights.

But I cannot think of life as I do,

Without influence of the best people,

The best places-I flew,

I make better art,

I make a better me after this,

As well as a better you.

And when we accept these beauties,

We're so coated,

We leave behind—

Gold residue.

There were cathedrals towered behind and before all of us.

This day was clean and seemed to go on forever.

The sky kept it's pale form that swallowed the clouds consistently, head-achingly.

And the lake was like a mirror, only we could see the stars beneath the tree-line.

We reached the shore.

It was beaten about and we weren't sure;

We contemplated going further to another island.

Only it would take too long, and we hadn't all day,

And the day was ultimately giving way.

Earlier I saw a flower near thick grass.

A single lily laying above the water.

I was tempted to bring it with me, as to bring it to her.

But it was rooted down to the shallow riverbed.

I couldn't take it from it's home

PART III

BEING HOMESICK ABOUT A PLACE

THAT IS NOT HOME

LOWERING EYELIDS

There,

One finds every bit of themselves.

They discover enough to fill a hundred shelves of literature

And then,

At least to me the idea seems most mature.

You arrive with no relationships

Not a single ship to harbor in the mind of anyone there.

No one knows one another and another bares

The answers to your philosophies and you bare theirs.

They're not destined to say it before you,

And I did not even know who they were yet.

Prior to them,

I found myself.

No influence but my own mind

That I'm left with so I see this place as a paradise

A place for me to redesign what I know as

The fundamentals of life,

The structure of everything and the result of even more.

I discover so much that I pray from the ceiling and look up at the floor

Like I'm adoring the confinement of the room

And the door is open—though I favor the window.

OUR EYES ARE SORE, FOR THIS GRAYISH SHORE

I find they're so

Interested in something about me,

Or about this place.

I place some words upon your marble,

You did not eat them.

The silence, you're late.

Some two-paged story that I threw into the black,

A pit in the spaced trees before the lake.

Some parties they held there and the water surged with noise

Colors melt into the water I poised around you—

Some evening the week prior.

Now the hundred others are gone,

And you and I can build our own fire,

Not of affection, love, or desire to relate

Not some fate *Twelve* told me about the other day.

But of ultimate discovery,

One's purest reason to proceed.

Not influenced by any other,

A man so intellectually perfect that God falls upon *his* knees.

Then God will see we have created him.

And he then created hope,

And that hope will soon kill us,

As we ignore the steepest slope.

If we conclude there is nothing greater than us tonight on the windy island

We could celebrate The End like some paradise that I can,

Or maybe I have already written about it.

Maybe I knew there is a solution to suffering before,

When I was young.

TANGERINE
𝔜𝔬𝔲 𝔯 𝔟𝔢𝔞𝔲𝔱 𝔬𝔲𝔱

I never once wished to close my eyes

And fall asleep forever like this

I have discovered some truths

There is not a single one that is pleasant

No bliss

But I can find this

In the whip of off-white clouds.

So much time for understanding our dimensions

I thought of them with her in my arms

I could tell there was so much tension

Yet there would not have to be

With Goddesses under my robes

Even they were not happy

When I'd wake up fully clothed

I dreamed

My face felt how it could cry

I would not show it in my eyes

No one would have to know

If I could figure it out

Maybe I would have enough time

But a king never tells royal lies

A mistress said I was much greater

But I was so increasingly deprived

I told the devil to leave later

I could see it in her eyes

Then I said in that dark crater

But for now

I'll pour a terrible wine

And a million kingdoms later

On her neck are golden lines

Come and see me later

Mary made me nearly fine

But she lied about the speed

Devils lie about the time

She said she needed me

As I work through her lies

My life was spent feeling better bodies

Breathing like a sleeping dragon

Smoking out of her big glossy eyes

There is fire in your eyes

Taking off that melting dress

You want me to be really sorry

Please do not take off that dress

There is something much brighter

I felt it on that island

The wind was much stronger

She said the stars look just like diamonds

She felt much more valuable

Malleable was one

Her body was an animal

Please

This isn't fun

Well that just isn't life.

And I've written it with a knife

Pain just isn't you

And it isn't right.

Three years and I didn't tell anyone of the roses and lilies.

I missed her!

Inside that tent I kissed her!

I know you're mad

I kissed darkness-

Is all she had

Until there was nothing left.

I missed her!

On that cliff I kissed her,

And I was worthless

But she found me

As she strips

I pulled her off

Her and her

I missed her!

She gave me all of these blisters!

I couldn't even say much

My mind stopped

My neck

My hands

She'd touch.

I missed her,

I loved,

Loathed,

And kissed her.

We got lost in the forest

We won't heal

And they all asked

But we're okay

RUSH BY OUR FEET

Diverine wasn't about you,

It was about her.

The luster,

Not the flower.

The Blonde who's so silent,

The one who laid with me on that island.

She was buoyant and loud,

Without releasing a sound.

Everybody loved you,

Even the pink clouds were stretching for you.

I shouldn't have consumed that pale purple and yellow,

It bursts in the sky and the water is shallow.

I remember that, I almost fell in,

The Blonde came over and told me to look within.

She says:

That flower was bad,

It was going to die anyways.

But I tried so hard to love her,

I tried for one thousand and ninety-five days.

A week to understand what I should do when I get home:

If I should stay drained,

Or finally be alone.

A lot would be happily done and they say it'll be easy,

But they don't know what she did.

TIGRE

Luscious silver and greens

Meet some salty leaked seas.

Near the water I lay by her

She's on her bruised nuclear knees,

And the skin is stained with earth.

Like the finale,

I finally found her.

We're warm in the grass

Breathing in the shivered flood

Ink drew leaves around her wrists

Drawn with red wine or her own blood.

I read *The Secret Garden* to her

As she falls asleep

All she sees is a blur,

Blurred figures

Wolves

A sinking ship

It is all we really were.

Salt embedded in our sweaters

Like flags above our heads.

I cannot remember a time

I loved you any more

Than when I dream

Without you in bed.

Your body feels cold

But you swear you are fine.

Maybe night will never come

And our demons will resign.

Let's lay by the coast

Exhaust the ship's lights away

Let's sleep in the long grass

We must be on our way.

Embroidered flowers

Flourish louder

Than what she could speak,

Dancing in cold showers

Poems allowed her,

She sang,

But she is still weak.

Weeks go by,

The grass had died.

Through it,

I have found her.

Resolutions subside,

In the party

I hide

Through it,

I see the Tiger.

DOUBLE NIGHT ISLAND

I dreamt I was between two Emerald Island Giants

Sitting and hunched over upon pearly-gazed marble floors,

Without the slightest reflection there and I had been there for four hours.

My legs hung under the water that had turned to glass at its face

That made me sore.

I bathed in the different colors of the day,

Blue in the morning

Red in the taste.

I waited for the idea of you,

Under the marble and between the green.

The nature before me was cobalt clashing

Silver and blues in the blades of rocks and trees.

But I was only dreaming of that house

With chrome floors that I would count,

I longed for that smoother place

And our heads laid and hair tangled about.

But we're not there and you wont talk

About anything but I didn't say a word,

Maybe I'd whistle but never shout.

Couldn't you see that place was just chaos?

Maybe you were scared of climbing that small cliff,

That maybe someone would wake up from some dream and would see us?

Because it wasn't too far into the night

They all had just seen the northern lights

They could've been awake,

That is okay that this is a dream

I meant to wake,

You up on that cliff I saw that shape.

Even you against that moon from that angle makes something in my chest quake

Even more-so my mind you make,

The idea of you is incredibly exciting.

I don't know why,

There were only three or four words between us.

I don't know why to me you were already beautiful,

And the others admired you also.

All there was,

Was the way you carried yourself

Like the dancer upon the moon named Apollo,

You float with every step.

You never talk,

You are quiet again,

I could never understand

Your motion.

Emotionless but you move fluently,

From what I can see you are fine.

Your voice reminds me of that first night on the island

The waves and your tongue speak so softly,

So fine.

Delicate were your words when you spoke them

In some accent you curled them,

I loved that you spoke them on time.

You all reside back in your tents,

There is no French that I could hear.

Just shifting trees and skinny rolling shores,

Those sounds were the most clear.

That day was open to anything and we were exhausted from the one before,

Canoeing across riptides and lakes,

Palming trees while rummaging through the woods with another

Left my hands and knees very sore.

I bled a lot from the branches that lined my chest

And stomach but I dared not to wear a shirt.

I had but one for the first four days

And the sun might have been really harsh

But eventually it wouldn't hurt.

But we grew so bored and reside to the picnic table out by the water.

There was just one more American,

A girl I'd seen before

She accompanied me on this trip.

The others spoke the same but different from her and I,

It seemed very odd and we agreed on it.

I imprinted our flag in the sand next to the table and the others dragged their feet upon it.

Hysterically we talked but something deeper in me had been disappointed.

Nothing came of noon,

There were only card games and swimming so I took an advantage.

With much of us quiet I pulled off my shoes,

Left them outside and resided into the tent

So that I may manage some extra rest.

I laid in a heap of clothes and sleeping bags whilst staring up at the roof of the tent,

It was ventilated and transparent so I looked up at the pastel sky.

Northern Manitoba was much more vibrant than home and then I close my eyes.

For an hour or two I dreamt of her and I

Residing on a hill of sand when the sky was golden before us,

And purple on the other side.

You lowered yourself upon me with your hair and your hands,

And your neck against my lungs

You beat upon my chest once.

I was not sure why,

With a hit I was left blue there and your body was still slow and seductive

But there was a feeling of a monster's hunt.

Like any dream there was no reason or motive

But I dreamt strictly of you,

And I was not sure if

It had been a nightmare or dream but I woke up with my hands on my head

And defeat rotting in my chest for some reason.

Stressed from the thought of you and the thoughts you bring me,

You made my mind experience every season.

I lay a little while longer in the tent,

Content until the blue above fills with patches of white.

Fulfilled with the days prior,

Having been so clear and cool,

We were prepared for any storm that may come our way.

My shirt was still in the tent and my shoes were outside of that.

Some trembling growling flooded from the woods

So we gathered inside the thundershack.

Backpacks piled in there,

Three walls so we could watch the lake lack-

The sun in two or three minutes.

The blond came over to me as I sat upon a table staring out at the beach

In English,

She said:

"I am finished."

Quiet and for me and decrypted oddly

I squinted my eyes,

"What do you mean?"

"Just come see me later,"

Some more words to add,

And that made me feel anxious

And a weird sort of glad.

Then the rain came down,

The world looked so low.

It rained much harder than the pace that I used to know.

I draped a black raincoat over my shoulders and thought:

I hope my shirt is in the tent and not on that rock

The one next to the table down by the beach

But I looked and there was nothing to see.

Nothing to admire of this place anymore

Not the people, noises,

Or Our Grayish Shore.

I surely believed it would rain until the next day

Or until the middle of the night.

But when would I see her?

The worry was right.

The rain beats harder but the sky is a little more bright.

Slightly mauve in patches.

You all were laughing in your group but we weren't,

We were quiet and watched the nature before us unfold.

In the back of the shack Wolfe talks to Maguire about some supposed story

"Never told."

Quickly they rush

The French without most of their clothes,

The air was cold but they ran to the water

We watched and observed their dance and splashing

All trying to discover their motive.

The French were interesting and not in a kind of way we could conclude.

No,

If,

They just were pleased with themselves and the water and the place

They thought they meant something in this dimension

And that nothing ever took up between space.

As if complications mean nothing,

But then I realized

That they understood something

And so,

I often waste my time.

If I can not see it

Then I waste my time.

TOO RAPID TO BEAR

That night felt like forever, headache pills and tremors, they storm our hearts, our fingers,

blisters, and begin to start—they all start rushing her.

Your heart just beats way too quick, your hands on me makes me sick, this was not about you.

But to me it is about you. Maybe I'm getting too much sleep.

When I wake up, I remember there is no such thing as fair. she's too fast, Too Rapid To Bear.

Save me, Blonde, I'll side with you. Forget that flower. I'll lay with you, For a while, not loving

You are not loving me—me still, I will never forget you, I just want to talk with you.

SEVEN TENTS

Violent had it been the wind on that island where the grass was long and grey

Where I arrived an hour later and I never saw you

One left

Talked to another and began to say;

This place is spacious,

You could reside right over there

As long as you do not bother us

Then we will not care.

The solid goldenrod tents set away from each other and sturdy

Though cold,

Underneath the ground was soft and the earth had spread

A wolf came and told me:

There she is!

I really could not believe it

I saw her across the field and under silvered skies

Magnificent was time and we could spend all of it

Like Kings rich with golden embroidery upon their heads

A crown upon mine no more

She reminded me of the devil who once said;

I forgot ever to cherish iridescence

We will be hopeless

And composed of evil's waiting essence.

Flavor of the island provided liberty to our chests

Dense of sweet yet so deprived of warmth

Inside the tent some stars just curl and sleep.

There I only was;

Sat upon a cliff over the threatening waters below

Alone when dinner had gone and the rapids churned very slow

Empty voices nourish people behind me.

I soaked in some beauty of a sunset I truly hadn't seen before

The French came next

Rested her head upon my shoulder.

I left for the tent when the rain pelted us

And I will never forget her.

I tried to convince myself our time was not spent

Some fluorescent waves rush above behind black clouds

S'il vous plaît ne laissez pas

Bloody Caesar soaks into her sweater.

ODYSSEY

The air is easy to breathe from the morning on the ketch

Salt fills it for me—Brought from the sea

Brought it from beneath the behemoth of scenes and what's so wretched leaves from the harbor.

And needn't god bother; for I and another— Live with stoicism and so by the shores we do

Ponder.

I let her get me-

Who had cut me off-

Here; Sin King, the wayward of:

Worn and I abandon my theodicy-

Along in sheets, her in robes,

Sitting above the palisades,

And therefore a new odyssey.

DRACO

After the Devil's party I leave to go to the hills that lower and lower to the belly of the valleys. I leave when the violets are violent; says dusk and the sky is purple and there's bleeding blues so much. I've yet to bring her there. I've yet to throw my tie over my shoulder, unbutton some, and I save myself for the peak of the hills' air—Colder there. But in three years she'll come to it.

ROSARY

Haven't we felt? And how could we feel each other if we're blatantly indifferent?
Indifference puts us in our place—us in our lives that're strange (if we're so far gone).
And why're we odd if we're thinking of higher things than the better who don't?
It's the better that would never decided whether not to think more and more, they just won't.
Poems of Huxley told me that maybe those who won't just can't.
Then I knew as a kid when I read them, I had to write my own while at camp.
And by the waves, the lowering me stays, I'm heavier and still afloat.
My idle life; I am surprised the meat of this is still sweet. I haven't tasted her fruit, just saw
orange by my eyes.
I haven't tasted but I knew. It is that we live through hell right up to July,
And I'm scared that you'd learn of life, and you'd certainly die knowing it.

RECEDE

Mine God, and my forging of beauty through art;

Is it all so beautiful? For, is it truly my composition?

If I have a billion, what would come after?

Why, if I'd take the billion, and my art is myself and we are the same beauty—

Have I reached the end?

And, am I troubled then?

If I sell my blood in my art and frame it with gold,

Have I reached the end?

What is life then and thereafter?

I must share laughs and wine with those who have nearly reached me,

And so-set on the violent sea.

Where'st the thunder of storms are days behind and before me—

My final goal begins to leave.

What is then after my goal?

Horizon, I am sure.

If I reach the ender after this limbo,

I may discover an ultimacy at the shore,

But I am sure this is the faint hope of my heart beginning to give in

To the finale of the sea.

I decide and create better divine emotions,

Where they can only be felt by witnessing the cold

And purple or gold days.

When ones body begins to halt in motion

They're alone and speechless to my newer divine ways.

In the stark of the open face of the mountain,

I think of too much that left me upon my knees.

If I act-to you-devout,

Maybe I can go back again, and recede without,

Mine God, and the forgéd beauty.

SUMMERED

Upon—Sleeping under the loud nature of moving trees and changing clouds,

We lay on vanilla sheets, ponder: how'd life go beyond that goal,

Beyond the nape of her neck, to laying on coal.

We're newly under stars-but on top-untold-I told her we'd be fine even when the hellish nights,

go,

We don't even need to fight as we never give up. As we're never enough, we're never fed up.

No, I may never wake up, if we lay in the cold of these summer nights,

When the smell of bonfires and the fade becomes bright: will something unfathomable come

From that-

Holy abyss or will the summer be comprised of something I missed.

When we watch the cobalt of the day melt into the gold of the evening,

I may fall into a love in which I enslave all of my demons.

And we summered Love,

She's coming on so fast,

The garden bed,

The season's last—they last not as long as the date—but as long as the weather.

One grows, another decides whether or not to be happy on sadistic neon nights-

And be beautifully okay under these tangerine street lights.

And beautifully done: our relations when we finally built with concrete,

Then beautifully demonstrated between lines of tall trees.

I've waited with blisters—my Love, I have kissed her.

I've waited the winter—beyond, and for sinners.

We; let us confide our beliefs to our wrists-I've strapped yours to my bed,

And I have been dying inside since I set foot on the beach.

And your curly hair covers what I kissed two weeks before: your forehead.

Violate melts with the pink above that you like—you reach to the headboard like you reach for

the sky,

For I told you everything must be all right, because if it isn't so, then we will not enjoy these

summer nights.

I've fought three already and I fight for the rest of my years: ideology: that liberation mixes well

with wine and tears.

It is the salt of the earth that I fear must be taken for more than a grain,

I see it like I see love and before you I'd refrain.

Before I had left and after the rain,

I stayed up with you-told me of darkening pain—but I told you everything is all right,

And then in these summer nights, I tell you I love this, and we can turn off the light.

The smell of cedar floods the room and smoke pours from the corners of my mouth and I hated-

When you did the same, because I knew you were younger and had no reason-

For being faded.

But love consumes us when we're opiated.

I wait by the lake for you, with the tea you solely stated-

Was the best.

But the taste burns the roof of my mouth quick,

And the tip of your tongue but it warms up my blood—maybe I won't become sick this time.

I wait by the lake for her,

Watching the hue of the sky change.

Watching you and then I change.

I fall to her godlessly,

Increasing my mountain of words for her-

And I recite to her the words of an odyssey.

I left for her colored, vibrance of crimson, cobalt, iridescence—I left her with one word.

These cooler nights,

Oh, how we Summered.

FERRY BEACH

In the fall, tired lions embroidered themselves along the goddess' arms.

In the summerly glow,

Soft-as-we-go

Wave caps sound a lot like psalms.

They sound a lot like songs, with the same pitch as her voice,

Like *Nuvole bianche*, when it truly destroys.

What is austere, what is vanilla unadorned, when she is even here?

When am I even around to hear the psalms—the ocean when it sways along-

The salt it steers my eyes-and there is no way that this could be wrong.

There is no way for this, and I think I missed the entire summer. mv,bC

And I think I kissed the devil, and I know I kissed the goddess,

And I know that there's a hundred-summoned thoughts beaming to their solace.

I knew they were mine,

I knew that two days was not enough time.

NEW ALEXANDRIA

"In the medieval times, I believe would be right, is when this was. The man, just five years older than me, lived in New Alexandria, a festive town that is very reminiscent of a luxurious and minimal English town, or the sweet settings within The Secret Garden. Just a very clean, mowed place with a massive castle and jolly villagers. But this man is not rich, and he isolates himself to his own paintings in a makeshift shack of a home. In his room, in the attic of it, where light comes through an ugly aperture in the roofing, he stands with a mounted canvas before him. Dry pigments of pinks and blondes are smeared across many canvases that he has leaned up against the sturdiest wall. I think it might be the best standing wall because the paintings support them. The money the man had, had been used for the building of the shack, and he had made the funds by selling his paintings to the elderly. But as they died, the new old had no desire for the man's paintings.

But his paintings, beautifully done, were influenced directly at the man's blazing interest in the King's daughter, of which, a figure so beautiful in the grace of her movement but also the natural value of her color. She was blonde and her skin was as fair as sand. She smiled the crescent of the moon, and she made the tides of the men very depleted. They desired her but refrained as they respected her noble appearance, but the man's entire life and ideas orbited around the contemplation of her. Sadly, as accurate as his paintings are, their eyes remain pale and white, for the man had never been close enough to the King's daughter to see the color of her eyes.

But one day it was rightfully so that the man concluded his secluded misery. In a near anger, the man travels into the wilderness south of New Alexandria in hopes to find the devil, so that he may come to terms with his desires and ultimately fulfill them.

So he finds the devil, of course, and makes a deal with him. It's that the princess will love him, in exchange for his life just twenty-four hours after she first makes eye contact with him.

The man runs to the village with extreme excitement, and tears running off of his face like rain. In the village there's a festival, in which the princess stands upon a pedestal while villagers sing and cheer. The scene is loud and happily executed.

Of course, the man is in the crowed and he sees her. Eventually she sees him and looks absolutely baffled. She fixates on him but she leaves as the festival draws to it's end. In the next hour, the man runs to the guards outside of the castle that the royals reside within. He requests to see the princess at the expense that they were once friends. The guard, who has never in his being encountered a conflict, nods and enters through a gate and proceeds into the castle. He comes back to the gate, leading the princess to the man. Her eyes widen and she runs to him. The guard opens the gate and the princess hugs the man. His knees weaken but stay locked when the man sees that her eyes were a bronze sort of brown. The princess tells the guard to tell her father that she had left with a friend. He does so, and the princess and the man run off into the woods near the man's shack.

As they laugh in love and wholesomeness, the man leads her to his shack to explain her immediate liking of him.

By the fire and the smoke rising into the hole in the ceiling, the man holds the princess, her blonde and all, as she cries about the devil.

Five hours go and the man falls limp beside his paintings alone and two hours later, an unattended fire and a young woman, at her sixes and sevens, leave the poor man.

Fire engulfs and exhausts through the aperture."

IT REALLY WAS A BEAR

It really was I that,

If thou art so intangible,

Purer than newer hate,

That is covered in-flammables.

If I may catch,

And if I must go,

I'd go on alone,

Without letting my Love know.

No,

She cannot know.

Today I go to the river,

And she cannot know.

When the water reigns red,

As crimson lines along the glass,

And my feet bury as they step on the river bed,

And the second sun begins to pass.

If I am wrong,

And I am impaired,

Then the nature is hellish,

And there really was a bear.

It really was I on the beach,

With the grace-named monster.

Not even a bleak day,

With the blue of the sky,

And blue of the water.

But blood shed from my elbows and shins,

The beast runs me from the woods and this begins.

I stand—my feet begin to sink into the sand.

It runs at me,

And treacherous shaking became of the land.

But as I hold-

My self to the beach and my glossed eyes glare,

I wait for my heated hands to save me again,

It really was a bear.

AS THERE IS NOT A BODY

As there is no longer myself

For myself to conquer.

For I have finished my spirit

But does she still wander?

Because it truly is her,

That this is about.

So I ponder: how could she do this to me, haven't I presented all I behold?

Is my revival of romanticism too much to be told?

I cannot tell her anymore,

She refuses it all.

She gets angry by it,

And refuses it all.

YOU WERE SATISFIED

Pink of it,

Whatever blossoms above falls in pieces to the long grass at my waist.

Before and behind is high and low land.

Oh, she holds my hand on the way.

In which I dreamt that if she had,

I would either have wasted the rest of my life,

Or been so blind to recognize it.

Oh, so I stay lone to the nature, on the cliff that overlooks dense low earth.

She sings how it means to her:

"Oh, the garden's smell and pristine lure!"

Greenery, trees, leaves, I'm breathing fumes as I leave me—

So behind me as I sit on the edge,

The verdant mane or a mural they depict as they surround me.

My palms remain open and subtle and exhausted as I finally conclude:

No, this isn't my home.

No, there never was,

A home below and above.

No art could ever save,

No hymn, moan, oh, they've—

Gone and left me down by the beach,

As dark comes, they've left me on my knees.

Obsidian of the sky at night when clouds enclave,

And swell to anchor my feelings.

I'm able to provide to her my sight and elite emotions,

And quickly, motions become slowly-moving-that are our elbows and legs so should I—

Give up notions of highness,

And then say good-bye to *real* art.

And say good-bye to myself,

And let beauty depart?

Because if nature cannot be wealth,

Then even more alone we die.

In riches heaped together dragging heaving from my lungs and bleeding ink,

Oh,

You were satisfied with

Leaving me out to die.

Oh,

But I'm better and unable to lie as

Purple twitches under my eyes,

My time was not wasted,

I answer my own questions-

As I open my eyes,

Six years ago.

I found a new art,

I found a new me,

I found a new sea to depart.

I lay as she picks me a-part.

I open my eyes,

I let art consume,

Because art was just not what I hung in these rooms.

Art was finding out the realities of life,

To not be so bothered when you think at night.

For I let my eyes strain,

As I let the cold of the tide-

Make me sound insane,

And make you satisfied.

I was gifted with everything there is to know about the mind. Now, I take materials, to keep me satisfied. Otherwise, I go. Since there is nothing left of life for me to figure out. I forgot about feelings a long time ago, when they became inefficient, and realities became valid.

I lay in an abode of beautiful catastrophes of the mind, the design, I did not create. I can only

thank the one who is not here,

For she persuaded me

    In the wilderness

    As I can see the end

    Behind me, leaving.

      I lay in an abode of riches, in an exhausted land

On a bed of blonde rapids,   at the end,   the grand

Il est cinq heures du matin

je me suis réveillé

Sur la colline, je vois le lac et le ciel irisé au-dessus et réfléchi

Mes yeux sont douloureux et l'air est frais

Je marche sur le chemin

Où elle a dit qu'elle attendrait

elle n'est pas là

Je pars une heure plus tard,

Parce que j'ai perdu tout un été